KT-438-614

Explorer 10   Rupert Furneaux

On Buried and Sunken Treasure

Illustrated by
Anthony Colbert

Puffin Books

2100034055

E.L.R.S.

S.

910.453

S115389.

Contents

The publishers and author would like to thank the following for their kind permission to reproduce the illustrations in this book:

Hart Davis Ltd, p. 26; Mary Evans Picture Library, p. 12; Fotolink, p. 24; Halifax Herald-Chronicle, p. 38; The Mansell Collection, p. 21; Nova Scotia Information Service, p. 36; Stanley Paul Ltd, pp. 18, 19; Pelican Publishing Co., Los Angeles, p. 7; Radio Times Hulton Picture Library, p. 10; Tom Stacey Ltd, p. 34; Stern, cover, title page, pp. 8, 24; Colin Summers and the U.S. Department of the Navy, p. 30; Tourist Photo Library, p. 20.

Puffin Books: a Division of Penguin Books Ltd, Harmondsworth, Middlesex, England
Penguin Books Inc., 7110 Ambassador Road, Baltimore, Maryland 21207, U.S.A.
Penguin Books Australia Ltd, Ringwood, Victoria, Australia

First published 1973

Text copyright © Rupert Furneaux, 1973
Illustrations copyright © Penguin Books Ltd, 1973

Made and printed in Great Britain by W. S. Cowell Ltd, 8 Butter Market, Ipswich

Set in 'Monophoto' Plantin

This book is sold subject to the condition that it shall not, by way of trade or otherwise, be lent, re-sold, hired out, or otherwise circulated without the publisher's prior consent in any form of binding or cover other than that in which it is published and without a similar condition including this condition being imposed on the subsequent purchaser.

All over the world people are searching for great and famous treasures –
concealed in the earth or lost in the depths of the sea.

Lives are risked; huge sums of money are spent. Some treasure has been
found. Still they dig and dive.

It is an exciting game, a challenge, because they are pitting their wits
against the men of long ago who did not intend their gold to be found.

The Florida Galleons

The eleven galleons making up the 1715 plate fleet straggled
through the Bahaman Passage, the narrow strait which separates
the Bahama Islands from the coast of Florida. Don Juan Esteban
de Ubilla, the Captain-General of the fleet, was anxious. His fleet
had sailed dangerously late from Havana, Cuba, the assembly port
in the Caribbean Sea. The hurricane season was close.

Every year, for two hundred years, the galleon fleet had sailed,
carrying to Spain the loot of the New World, the gold, silver and
jewels plundered from the mines of Mexico and Peru. The annual
'trade', as it was called, amounted to several million pounds, an
even greater sum in modern dollars. This year's cargo was greater
than usual. Due to the long war in Europe, and danger from enemy
fleets, the treasure had piled up awaiting shipment.

Don Esteban had an even greater worry. He carried in his own
flagship a very special cargo, the magnificent collection of jewels
ordered by his master, the Spanish King, as a wedding gift for his
bride, the Duchess of Parma. This fortune in gems included a
necklace made of 128 matched pearls, and another formed of three
strands of gold, eleven feet (3·35 metres) in length and weighing
half a pound (226 grammes).

The top-heavy, cumbersome galleons were loaded to the gun-
wales. Don Esteban's flagship, the *Nuestra Senora del Carmen Y*
San Antonio, the one-time *Hampton Court*, which had been
captured from the English, led the fleet.

The dangerous Bahaman Passage was the only seaway from the
Caribbean in sailing ship days. The prevailing easterly winds pre-
vented ships from returning to Europe by the way they had come
through the island chain encircling the sea. The Bahaman Passage
had been the graveyard of many rich galleons. Caught by hurricanes

3

within its narrow strait, hundreds of ships had been lost on the Bahaman reefs and the Florida Keys. One minute there would be blue sky, a gentle wind, calm sea; the next, a howling gale, mountainous seas and – disaster. Caught in the grip of cyclonic winds, the towering, unwieldy galleons stood no chance.

At sunset on the night of 30 July 1715 the fleet lay becalmed. A slight haze shrouded the glassy sea; low clouds loomed on the horizon. The flock of birds swarming in the ships' wake took off, making for the shore twenty miles away. Don Esteban shivered in the hot and sultry night, for these were the signs of hurricane.

It struck the fleet at dawn the next day. The helpless galleons were engulfed in foaming waves, battered by the howling gale. Sails were wrenched from the toppling masts, and the galleons were driven shorewards, battered wrecks. Ten galleons were cast upon the Florida reefs, and one thousand seamen drowned. A few hundred scrambled up the beach. Only one ship escaped: she limped back to Havana carrying tidings of the terrible disaster, the worst in the history of the Spanish plate fleet.

Salvage teams and soldiers were sent to Florida. The Spaniards conscripted a tribe of Indians. The Indians were carried over the reefs in skiffs, given casks to put over their heads – primitive diving bells – weighted with a stone, and told not to surface without treasure. Braving sharks, barracudas and the danger of drowning, they scoured the seabed, and in four years recovered about one third of the lost treasure, at the cost of the lives of the whole tribe.

The Spaniards collected the salvaged cargoes in the fort they had built in the dunes. It was attacked by the English pirates who swarmed to the disaster scene. One captain from Jamaica, Henry Jennings, stole 350,000 silver coins.

The loss of the 1715 plate fleet became a famous legend. I heard it when I visited Florida before the Second World War. The treasure galleons, it was thought, had become submerged in mud and sand, twenty fathoms deep. Out at sea lay a fortune in sunken gold. Its recovery was just a dream in those days of heavy diving suits and air compressors.

Then three things happened: the aqualung and skin-diving equipment were invented, and their perfection made underwater exploration and salvage possible by amateur divers; the Florida coast was struck by a heavy storm; and, even more important, Kip Wagner arrived. He came to live on the Florida coast, at Sebastian

Creek, half way between Daytona Beach and Miami, shortly after the end of the Second World War. He worked at house building and decorating, and in his spare time joined the beachcombers who scoured the shore line, looking for debris thrown up by the great storm. One day Wagner picked up a blackened, coral-encrusted lump, and breaking it open, he found a clump of coins.

Kip Wagner noticed one significant fact. All the coins were inscribed PHILIP V. BY THE GRACE OF GOD 1714, and they had been minted in Mexico and Peru. None were dated later than 1714, the year before the sailing of the lost plate fleet.

Wagner had, of course, heard the legend of the disaster. The storytellers told two different tales: one said the galleons had been lost 50 miles (80 km) to the north, another stated they had gone down 120 miles (193 km) to the south of Sebastian Creek. Of one thing everyone was certain – they had not been wrecked off Sebastian Creek. Wagner's coins had travelled a long way.

A section of the map drawn in 1775 by Bernard Romans, showing Sebastian Creek.

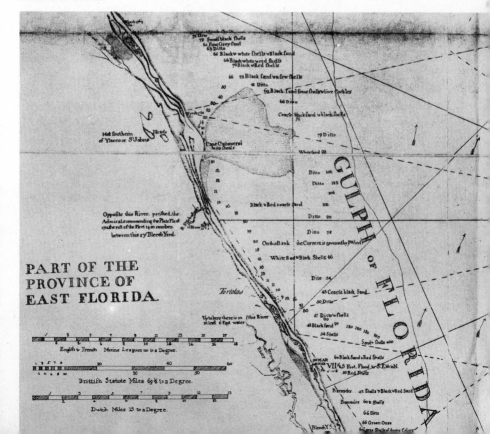

Wagner showed his find to his doctor friend, Kip Kelso. As it happened, Kelso was about to visit Washington, and he promised to search at the Library of Congress to learn, if possible, where the plate fleet *had* been wrecked. Kelso found a book, too rare and precious for display. Written in 1775 by the English map-maker, Bernard Romans, it was called *A Concise Natural History of East and West Florida*. Its author had surveyed the coast only sixty-four years after the famous disaster. What was more, he had drawn a map of the east coast. It carried these words:

Opposite this river perished the Admiral commanding the Plate Fleet of 1715, the rest of the Fleet fourteen in number, between this and the bleach yard.

Romans had picked up Spanish coins on the beach. The local Indians, the descendants of the drowned divers, had misinformed him only about the number of galleons that had been lost.

Romans's early history had been forgotten or ignored by the host of treasure hunters who had dreamed and talked of recovering the plate fleet's gold. Only Kelso and Wagner *knew* where the 1715 galleons had sunk. Ten plate ships had gone down right opposite Wagner's home by the Sebastian Creek – out at sea from the beach where he had found the coins dated 1714.

Neither Wagner nor Kelso were skin divers, so Wagner paddled out to sea precariously balanced on an inflated tyre tube. Peering into the depths, he saw strange shapes, ancient anchors and cannon. The same storm that had thrown up the coins had bared them of the sand of centuries. Stretching away southwards lay the bones of nine other wrecks.

A skin-diver collecting treasure from the ocean floor.

Wagner set about recruiting a team of skilled skin divers. He found it ready-made – the Aqua Lung Club, formed by the Space technicians of Cape Kennedy. While Wagner organized the search, Kelso visited the Archives of the Indies at Seville in Spain. In this maze of ancient records he found the actual bills of lading, the cargo manifests, of the 1715 plate fleet, eye-witness reports made by the survivors of the disaster, and the records kept by the salvagers. The lost galleons were named, their cargoes registered, their death-beds indicated. Their registered cargo amounted to $14,000,000. That was probably only half the total, for all galleon captains carried secret, unregistered treasure.

While awaiting the purchase of a salvage boat the team explored the dunes, searching for the salvagers' base camp. Wagner's dog provided the clue. It drank from a stagnant pool – proving it to have been the camp's well. Wagner scoured the ground, armed with an old war-time mine-detector. He unearthed numerous coins, all dated 1714. One of the team made an even more remarkable discovery: the three-strand golden necklace intended for the Spanish King's bride. It has been valued at $50,000.

In ten years the Real Eight Corporation, as they call themselves, have dredged 60,000 coins valued at $3,000,000 from the sea-bed, many pieces of eight (each today worth $10–$20), and golden doubloons (each worth $150–$200). They have found also gold and silver ingots, a silver dinner service, and a twenty-eight-piece porcelain tea service, together worth another million dollars. The tea service had been imported to Mexico from China.

The Real Eight Corporation divers have located all ten galleons. They have acquired from the State of Florida exclusive right of search. Many years of hard work lie ahead, and they fear only that another great storm may once again cover the wrecks in deep layers of sand and mud.

Kip Wagner's discovery of the lost plate fleet is the great modern epic of treasure trove. He found the galleons because he and Kelso went back to the earliest source of information – something no one else had bothered to do.

For further reading:
Kip Wagner, L. B. Taylor, *Pieces of Eight*, Dutton, 1966.
Dave Horner, *The Treasure Galleons*, Dodd, Mead, 1971.

Captain Kidd's Golden Hoard

Captain Kidd is *the* famous pirate of all pirates. Everyone *knows* that he concealed a huge treasure. He said so himself. In consequence, people have been looking for it for two hundred years. Two friends of mine believe they know where it lies concealed, but they have picked two different places, ten thousand miles apart. They cannot both be right.

The search for Kidd's treasure is almost a story-book tale. But not quite so simple.

First, who was Kidd? He may have been born in Scotland about 1645. We hear of him first in New York in 1689, when he married a rich widow, Sarah Oort. In the marriage register he is described as 'WILIAM KIDD. GENTLEMAN'. Kidd is thought to have been a merchant, the owner-captain of a vessel trading with the West Indies. He was certainly there in 1691. He commanded a privateer, a ship licensed by the government to seize enemy vessels in wartime. Kidd's crew, many of whom had been pirates, seized the ship, stranding him on shore. He had probably refused to turn pirate himself.

We hear next of Kidd in 1695. He travelled to London, where he was commissioned by King William III to 'clear out the nest of pirates' who preyed upon ships in the Indian Ocean, but Kidd was cautioned against 'molesting our friends and allies at his peril'.

Kidd was backed by a number of important men, the First Lord of the Admiralty, the Lord Chancellor, the Lord Keeper of the Great Seal, and the Master-General of the Ordnance. They found the money to pay for the voyage, obviously hoping to make

10

a large profit. Kidd himself would receive a percentage of the profits, as would his crew. This 'no prey, no pay' system was adopted by privateers and pirates. It meant that if no prizes were taken, no one would make any profit. The crew received no pay, only a share of the loot.

Kidd sailed his *Adventure Galley*, 287 tons and 34 guns, to New York. There he increased his crew to 170 men by embarking a number of rogues – some of the very pirates he had been ordered to capture.

Kidd sailed across the Atlantic and into the Indian Ocean, to the island of Madagascar, the famous pirate haunt, but finding no pirates there, he sailed on to the coast of India in search of prizes. England and France were at war, so French ships were fair prizes.

For a whole year Kidd made no captures. Furious at their captain's lack of success, the crew became mutinous. The *Adventure Galley*'s gunner, a man named Moore, threatened Kidd. Acting correctly as the Captain of a ship carrying the King's Commission, Kidd seized a bucket and struck Moore on the head, breaking his skull. Kidd's quick action ended the mutiny, for the time being.

Continuing his voyage, Kidd sighted the *Quedah Merchant*, a richly laden ship belonging to the Great Moghul, the ruler of India. Kidd seized the vessel on the excuse that she sailed under a pass issued by the French king, which made her a legitimate prize of war. But Kidd failed, as his commission required, to bring his prize into a British port. Instead he sailed her to Madagascar. There he found a number of pirates, including Captain Culliford, one of the men he had been sent to capture.

Making no attempt to arrest these pirates, Kidd shifted his guns to the *Quedah Merchant*, abandoning his old vessel, and sailed to the Dutch East Indies, the islands of Java and Sumatra, where he learned that he had been proclaimed an 'obnoxious pirate'.

Kidd, it seems, had been overpowered by his mutinous crew. That was the story heard by Lord Bellomont, the Royal Governor of New York, who informed Kidd's backers on 15 May 1699:

I am in hopes the several reports we have here of Captain Kidd being forced by his men against his will to plunder two Moorish ships [meaning the ship owned by the Great Moghul] may prove true, and it is said one hundred of his men revolted from him at Madagascar and were about to kill him when he absolutely refused to turn pirate.

We hear again of the *Quedah Merchant* in the West Indies, where Kidd abandoned her. He went to New York to clear his name, taking the French passes he had found on that ship. Lord Bellomont promised Kidd protection for himself and his treasure, which was stated to be worth £40,000 – something like £500,000 in present-day money. But Kidd appears to have doubted Lord Bellomont's word, and hid £14,000 on Gardiner's Island in New York harbour.

Kidd's suspicions of Bellomont proved only too true. The Governor dug up Kidd's money, clapped him in irons and sent him to London for trial as a pirate.

Kidd's trial was a 'frame-up'. His powerful backers, to whom he had brought no profit, deserted him, fearing that they might be charged with aiding and abetting him in his alleged misdeeds, and Kidd failed to produce the French passes which might have proved his innocence. They had been taken from him by Lord Bellomont and sent to London. They were found in the Public Record Office only a few years ago.

Kidd was charged with piracy and with the murder of gunner Moore. He refused to defend himself on the piracy charge, relying on the lost passes, but despite the well-recognized right of a Captain to use violence to quell mutiny, he was convicted of Moore's murder and condemned to be hanged at Execution Dock, Wapping.

Captain Kidd before the bar at the House of Commons.

While awaiting execution in Newgate Gaol, Kidd wrote a letter to the Speaker of the House of Commons:

In my proceedings in the Indies, I have lodged goods and Tresure to the Value of one hundred thousand pounds, which I desiere the Government may have the benefit of, in order thereto I shall desiere no manner of liberty but to be kept prisoner on board such Shipp as may be appointed for that purpose and only give the necessary directions and in case I faile therein I desiere no favour but to be forthwith Executed according to my Sentence.

The government refused Kidd's plea, believing probably that his offer was no more than an excuse to gain stay of execution. The money found on Kidd, £6,473, was used to found Greenwich Hospital.

Kidd's last words are the only *evidence* that he concealed treasure until the nineteen-thirties, when a number of strange discoveries were made.

A retired lawyer, living in Eastbourne, Sussex – Hubert Palmer – bought a heavy oak bureau, which bore a brass plate inscribed *Captain William Kidd, Adventure Galley, 1669.* That was the name of the ship Kidd commanded in 1695. Fiddling about with the chest, Palmer discovered a secret compartment. In it he found a chart of an island, bearing the words '*China Sea*', the date 1669 and the initials 'W.K.'. There was no clue to the island's location. Palmer traced and bought three more 'Kidd' relics, two sea chests and a box, inscribed '*William and Sarah Kidd. Their Box*'. All three contained secret compartments, each providing charts of the same island.

Two of these charts were far more detailed than the others. They supplied compass bearings, latitude and longitude, and showed hills, woods, valleys, coral reefs and a lagoon. One chart depicted 'two wrecks' off-shore. Both charts carried sets of directions which, though different, appeared to indicate the stepping out of a course.

These charts were examined by an expert at the British Museum who described them as genuine seventeenth-century charts. Comparison between specimens of Kidd's handwriting and the lettering on the charts indicated that both had been written by the same hand.

I have seen these charts. They seem to be treasure charts, for places are marked with a cross, and the route to be followed is indicated by dots; but the directions given do not seem to fit the markers. The only clues to the island's location are the words '*China Sea*' and the latitude and longitude, which indicate that part of the world.

An ex-naval officer believes he has identified Kidd's island in that area. It is shown on ancient charts drawn before Kidd's time. Perhaps Kidd visited the China Sea in his youth, in 1669. Did he then have treasure to hide?

I think it more likely that he stole some other pirate's secret, perhaps while he was on a trading voyage to the West Indies. The date he put on his charts may be significant, for 1669 was the year when the famous buccaneers were ousted from their stronghold on the island of Tortuga, on the north coast of modern Haiti. Maybe they hid their treasures elsewhere, and Kidd overheard their talk. That could account for the lack of precision in the charts he drew in order to memorize the information he had gained. He did not know where the island lay. That may be why, late in life when he was a prosperous merchant, and a happily married man, he accepted a commission to go on a dangerous venture (which

The Kidd-Palmer chart found in 'William and Sarah Kidd, their box'.

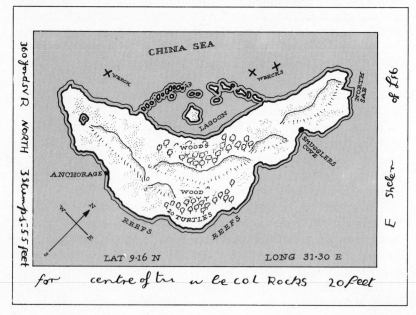

14

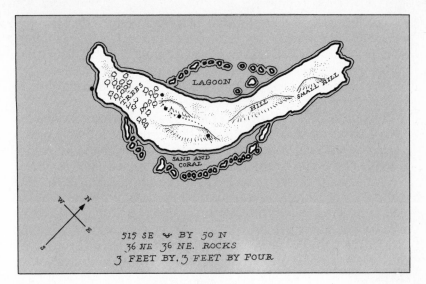

The Kidd-Palmer chart found in the sea chest.

proved fatal) to take him to the Indian Ocean and the East Indies – where he believed the buccaneers' treasure had been concealed. Alas, we shall never know. The Kidd charts refuse to yield the vital secret.

Other famous pirates may have concealed their treasures. Blackbeard Teach buried his wealth on the coast of North Carolina, close to the house he had built behind Plum Point on the Pamlico river. One night in 1716 his ship, the *Revenge*, anchored off the point. Teach led the way up the beach, followed by six of his men carrying shovels and a great iron-bound chest. They dug a vault and buried the chest, refilling the hole under Teach's watchful eye. Within a few days the six men were dead; Teach was killed two years later. Yet, someone inherited his secret. On Christmas Day, 1928, two trappers in search of game stumbled on a freshly dug hole. Leading from it were the footsteps of three men, and the marks left by the chest as they had dragged it to the near-by river. Somehow they had found the exact spot where Teach had buried his gold.

Sir Henry Morgan, the famous buccaneer, may have concealed part of the loot he gained from his sack of the Spanish city of Panama in 1671. He missed many of the city's treasures, for the

15

citizens, learning of his approach, concealed some of their possessions in subterranean tunnels beneath the city. Using a metal detector, the English naval lieutenant, George Williams, unearthed golden goblets, a silver church bell, a golden, jewel-encrusted crucifix, golden utensils and coins in 1936. These are exhibited in the city's museum.

The pirate author, Esquemeling, says that Morgan cheated his men of their fair share of the spoil, hiding part of it on his return journey. What may have been Morgan's gold was found by chance in 1935. The English explorer, Frederick Mitchell-Hedges, found five iron-bound chests concealed in a cave on the island of Roatan, in the Gulf of Honduras, a famous pirate harbour. He is believed to have taken away treasure valued at £100,000. But he was forced to leave one chest behind. When another expedition visited the cave in 1965, the chest had gone. That is all we know. People who find treasure keep quiet. Successful searches are cloaked in secrecy.

For further reading:
H. T. Wilkins, *Captain Kidd and his Skeleton Island,* Cassell, 1935.
A. D. Howlett, 'The Mystery of Captain Kidd's Treasure' *World Wide Magazine,* October 1958.

The Treasure of the Tuamatos

A coral island. A pear-shaped pool. In its depths tons of gold, guarded by sea monsters, a giant octopus and a moro-eel. And the way to the treasure is shown on the proverbial sea-stained chart. What more can you want?

The story starts in 1849. The Church at Pisco, a town on the coast of Peru, housed great treasure: golden ingots, golden candlesticks and ornaments, and rich jewels. It weighed 14 tons and had been stolen originally from the Incas, the ancient people of that part of South America, whom the Spaniards had conquered and enslaved.

The priests of Pisco guarded their treasure jealously. They hid it in a deep underground vault, protected by iron bars. No thieves, however audacious, could break in to steal it, and no one, except the priests, knew it existed.

The first link in the chain of security was broken when one priest, Father Matheo, ran away to sea. He told the secret of the treasure to a rogue named Diego Alvarez, who brought three other men into the plot: Brown, Barnett and Killorain. They went to Pisco, where Alvarez and Killorain, both good Catholics, impressed the priests by their show of godliness. Alvarez told the senior priest that the one-time Father Matheo was on his way to Pisco with a gang of rogues to steal the treasure.

But there was not time to send to the Peruvian capital for soldiers. The good Fathers, fearful for their gold, believed Alvarez. What could they do to safeguard it? Alvarez had his answer ready: he and his friends would take it to the Peruvian capital – under guard by priests. The Fathers fell for this bare-faced trick. The treasure was loaded on to the *Bosun Bird*, the ship hired by Alvarez, and the voyage commenced. As soon as they were safe from view the gang knocked the priests on the head and threw them overboard. But what could they do with the £3,000,000 worth of treasure? Obviously the thieves could not land it at any port, for they were unable to account for its ownership. Once again Alvarez had a ready answer. They would sail across the Pacific, land on a remote, uninhabited South Sea island and hide the treasure temporarily. They would then sail on to Australia and give

The Tuamatos.

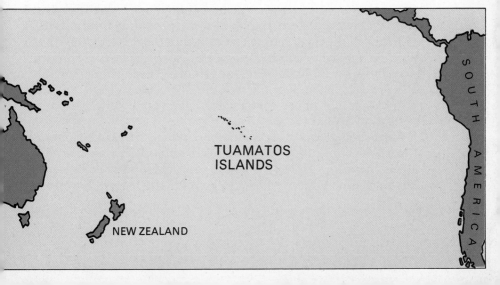

TUAMATOS
ISLANDS

NEW ZEALAND

SOUTH AMERICA

George Hamilton on Fakarava Atoll, site of the treasure lagoon.

themselves out as ship-wrecked mariners. They could then hire another ship and return to the island.

Unfortunately for them it did not work out like that. Alvarez, Barnett and Brown were killed in a brawl shortly after they arrived in Australia, some time about 1850, and Killorain was sent to prison for his part in the fight. But he was now the sole owner of the map Alvarez had drawn, showing where the treasure had been hidden.

On his release, twenty years later, Killorain became a tramp. One night, old and weary, he came to a shack. Its owner gave him food and shelter. On his death-bed Killorain told his secret to this man – Charles Edward Howe.

Armed with Killorain's map, Howe sailed to the Tuamatos islands (part of French Tahiti), where Killorain had told him to look for a tiny island, marked by a coral pinnacle on its eastern shore. Howe landed on what he thought to be the island shown on the map. He lived there from 1910 to 1927, digging for treasure. It took him all these years to realize that coral islands look very much alike. He moved to another island and, so the story goes, immediately found the Pisco treasure – or part of it. He dug up a chest filled with jewels. The bulk of the treasure, the golden ingots, Killorain said, had been dropped into a pear-shaped pool. Howe gazed into its murky depths.

What should he do? He could not recover the treasure alone, but if he spoke of his discovery the French authorities would seize the stolen treasure. Howe re-buried the chest, and returned to Australia, where he tried to find backers and helpers for another

18

The pool and scene of operations just before sinking the coffer dam.

voyage to lift the treasure. He showed Killorain's map to prove his story.

Howe found men ready to search for the treasure, but mysteriously he disappeared before they could organize the voyage, and was never seen again. He had handed over his map though.

Howe's partners went about the treasure hunt in the right way. They made inquiries in the Tuamatos islands and in Peru; yes, they were told, Howe had spent years digging for treasure; yes, the church of Pisco had been robbed of its treasures; yes, the *Bosun Bird* had reached Australia. The partners secured from the French Government permission to dig for treasure in the Tuamatos. They came to London to raise additional money, and to find a diver, a man to bring up the golden ingots from the depths of the pear-shaped pool: young George Hamilton answered the advertisement and joined the party.

The six adventurers voyaged to Tahiti, hired a schooner and looked for an island marked by a coral pinnacle. They found it at last and hurried ashore. Within a few minutes they were standing by the pear-shaped pool, exactly as Killorain and Howe had described it. This pool was close to the beach and was tidal, being connected to the sea far below the surface.

The partners probed the depths of the pool with drills. Below twelve feet (3·6 metres) of water they went into six feet (1·8 metres) of sand. At one spot they struck something hard. Hamilton put on diving gear and went down to investigate. He felt a tug on his ankle: he was in the grip of a giant octopus, its tentacles encircling his body. He plunged his diver's knife into its body, and was engulfed in stifling darkness – the inky fluid ejected by the monster. Hamilton shot to the surface.

He dived again. This time he was attacked by a moray-eel, its body the thickness of a man's thigh, its jaws armed with jagged teeth. He fought it off and surfaced again.

The pool was freed at last from its sea-monster guardians, thought the adventurers. Now they could get at the treasure.

But they faced another problem. If they were to find the gold which they believed lay hidden deep in the sand, it would have to be dug out by hand. They built and lowered a 'coffer-dam', a makeshift device to hold back the sand as they dug downwards. But it failed to work: each time the diver emptied it, it refilled with sand.

Far better equipment would be required before they could reach the treasure. To build or buy it would take time and more money. The partners failed to raise this, and so they were forced to abandon their search for the gold of Pisco.

Does it lie still in the depths of the pear-shaped pool?

For further reading:
Charles Nordoff, *Faery Lands of the South Seas*, 1933.
George Hamilton, *The Treasure of the Tuamatos*, Hutchinson, 1938.

A moray eel.

Sir William Phips as Governor of
Massachusetts.

Phips's Galleon

No lost and sunken treasure has been more eagerly sought than
the *bulk* of the rich cargo of the Spanish plate ship, the *Nuestra
Senora de la Concepcion*. She sailed from Havana, Cuba, in 1659,
carrying 100 tons of bullion, chiefly silver, from the mines of
Mexico. She was dismasted and crippled in a hurricane. Her
commander, Admiral Juan de Villavicencio, struggled to get his
ship to Hispaniola – another Spanish island, the modern Haiti – but
his efforts were in vain. The *Concepcion* struck the Los Abrojos
reef and sank in 30 feet (9 metres) of water. Some survivors reached
Hispaniola, and one sailor claimed he knew where the treasure
galleon had been wrecked amongst the mass of jagged reefs
60 miles (96·5 km) to the north.

William Phips, a ship's carpenter on a vessel trading from the
British colony of Massachusetts to Hispaniola, heard the story of
the famous galleon, and listened to the old sailor's tale. The sailor
said that the *Concepcion* had sunk close to a pillar of rock, easily
visible above the mass of shoals and sea-washed reefs. This was a
tremendous clue. Without it, all search for the lost galleon in that
uncharted sea would be hopeless. Phips had no ship of his own and
no money, but he took himself to London and talked his way into
the presence of the King, the gay and extravagant Charles II.

Charles, himself hard-up for money, listened to Phips's wonder-
ful tale. He alone, Phips pretended, knew the site of the famous
galleon's wreck. His bluff worked. Charles loaned him a ship in
return for a quarter share of any treasure Phips might find.

Phips set off in the *Rose* in 1683. Reaching the scene of the wreck,
he was horrified to see several vessels 'fishing' for the *Concepcion*'s

gold. Their captains, too, had heard the old sailor's yarn. Believing they were too late, the crew of the *Rose* mutinied, demanding that Phips turn pirate. Phips knocked down the ringleaders with his bare fists, quelling the mutiny. He sailed his ship to Jamaica, handed over his crew to the governor, and shipped another gang of rogues. He returned to Hispaniola, where he found the Spanish sailor again. He gave Phips more detailed information, enabling him to draw a chart of the reefs. But that alone was not enough to enable Phips to find the galleon. He would have to fight off the other searchers, desperate men who would laugh at his Royal Commission.

Phips returned to England. Charles II was dead, and his successor, James II, refused to loan the warship Phips craved. But Phips's story came to the ears of several rich and powerful men, and they fitted out three ships for him, two of them heavily armed. One was commanded by Francis Rogers, who had been Mate of the *Rose*. Phips set out once again on his treasure quest.

He reached Hispaniola in December 1686. He seems to have been unsure of his clues, for he sent Rogers in the 50-ton ship, the *Henry*, to start the search. Phips lingered at the island's chief harbour, Porto Plata, living in his large and better-armed vessel, the *James and Mary*.

Rogers spent three weeks on the reefs. On the first day out, he and a diver had paddled over the reefs in a canoe. On their way back the diver noticed a beautiful sea-plant rising from the coral. He dived to get it, and reappeared quickly with the exciting news that close by the plant lay several 'great guns'. He had found the *Concepcion*. Sent down again, the diver brought up bars of silver and some pieces of eight; during the next few days divers recovered 3,000 pieces of eight and more silver bars. Rogers returned to Porto Plata, where he found Phips in despair and talking of giving up the search. He invited Rogers to join him at dinner. Rogers did not let on about his find, and waited until Phips was busy eating. Then he slipped a silver bar beneath the table where Phips could not fail to see it. 'Why? What is this?' he cried, 'Thanks be to God. We are made.'

The difficulty in finding the *Concepcion* was explained. The old sailor's 'pinnacle of rock' had become encrusted by coral, and within a few years the wreck itself would have become unrecognizable beneath layers of coral.

The great underwater treasure hunt began on 16 February 1687. Leaving their ships at anchor, at safe distance from the dangerous reefs, Phips and Rogers rowed their divers over the wreck. Over a period of weeks the divers brought up ingots of gold and silver, chests and bags of coins, which had become scattered on the sea bed. But the real treasure lay trapped in the hull, secure in the plate-room. How to get it out?

Phips proved to be an ingenious treasure-hunter. His divers secured a barrel of gunpowder to the wreck. He obtained hollow reeds from Hispaniola, which were thrust down into the sea, one fitting into another, to provide a watertight covering for the cotton fuse placed within. But each time Phips lit the fuse, the cotton burned the reeds and the water poured in. Try as he might, he could not explode the gunpowder.

Phips had done his best with the primitive tools available in those days. He returned to England carrying treasure which was valued at £300,000 (£1,000,000 in present-day money). He received £12,000, was knighted by the King, and sent to Massachusetts as Royal Governor. But his two-fisted methods of ruling his subjects led to his recall to England, where he died on 18 February 1694.

Meanwhile a host of craft had gathered at the Silver Shoals, as the wreck-site had been named in honour of Phips's exploit. Several captains reaped rich rewards from the sea bed, scooping up the treasure Phips had been forced to leave behind. Treasure valued at £47,000 was landed at Bermuda alone, but, like Phips, these 'fishers' failed to burst into the *Concepcion*'s hull.

No one knows how many people have tried to wrest the bulk of the cargo from the *Concepcion*'s wreck. Armed with modern explosives and skin-diving equipment, they could do that easily – if they could find the galleon again, but her timbers must have decayed years ago, and by now she must have become encrusted with many feet of coral.

A. H. Verrill, an experienced treasure hunter, came to the Shoals in his own yacht in 1932. He had studied the logs of Phips's ships, hoping to find clues to the *Concepcion*'s site. Verrill, gazing through the clear water, saw cannon lying on the sea bed, sure signs of an ancient shipwreck. His divers traced its outline, but, lacking explosives, they could do no more than tap the encrusted coral. Verrill returned to what he thought was the site in 1934, and again located

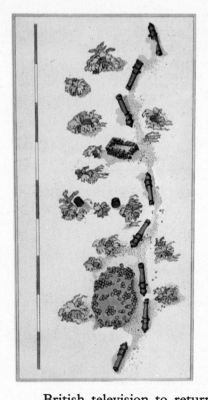

the *Concepcion*, but his explosive charges were not sufficiently powerful to blow away the encrusted coral, now fully two feet (599 mm) thick.

Several teams of American frogmen are believed to have visited the Silver Shoals since the Second World War. And in 1967 the French underwater expert, Alexandre Korganoff, told the *Sunday Mirror* that he had definitely located the famous wreck. Following a careful study of Phips's papers and the chart he had drawn, preserved in the Public Record Office, he had sailed to the site with the late Profirio Rubirosa, Dominican diplomat and famous playboy. But 'haunted by the presence of the treasure which they thought they could pick out of the water below', the crew, Korganoff said, 'tried to get rid of us'. Rubirosa sailed his yacht to Jamaica, where the mutinous crew were put in prison.

Korganoff announced his plans on British television to return to the wreck, in which he believes £50,000,000 awaits discovery.

Yet another treasure hunter visited the site in 1967. The English yachtsman, Ted Falcon-Barker, also believes he has located the *Concepcion*, and he has tracked her course through the reefs. It is marked by the cannon thrown overboard by the crew. The *Concepcion* almost escaped from the reefs. She lies, now, close to deep water, overhanging a cleft in the rocks, still thickly encrusted with coral. Falcon-

Opposite page: The *Concepcion*, Phips's galleon.
Left: Diagram showing how the *Concepcion*'s 'great guns' lay scattered on the sea floor.
Right: Visual explanation of how a sunken galleon shifting in the sand spills out its treasure.

24

This medallion was struck in honour of Phips in 1687. Fishing symbolizes fishing for treasure – the date 1686 was inscribed to commemorate the Society of Gentlemen Adventurers.

Barker dived down and brought up gold coins and a life-size golden finger-nail, part, he thinks, of a golden statue.

As far as is known neither Korganoff nor Falcon-Barker has returned to the reefs. No doubt both would like to have another go at recovering the treasure.

Someone, some day, may re-locate the *Concepcion* and, using gelignite, blow open her plate-room. If they do that, the ship's vast wealth will be theirs alone. The galleon sank outside territorial waters, thus no government can claim a share of the lost treasure, not even the Spaniards: they have let it go by default.

For further reading:
C. H. Karraker, *The Hispaniola Treasure*, O.U.P., 1934.
A. H. Verrill, *They Found Gold*, Putnam, 1936.
T. Falcon-Barker, *Devil's Gold*, McKay, U.S.A., 1967

The Treasures of Cocos Island

Should you need to bury treasure, you could not find a better place anywhere in the world than Cocos Island. It is remote, inaccessible, uninhabited, a tiny speck in the Pacific Ocean, 350 miles west of Costa Rica. It is the scene of one of the world's greatest treasure hunts.

The story is typical of treasure trove. The many searchers have kept their information secret; the vital map is lost; the clues have become hopelessly mixed. Earthquakes have destroyed the island's landmarks, the signs that lead to the secret cave. This can only be found again by dynamiting and bulldozing the mass of rock and earth which may cover its ingenious door.

Two treasure hunters once found and entered that cave. Only one came out. The skeleton of the other remains there to this day – the silent guardian of the loot of Lima.

The story starts in 1821. That was the year when the people of South America rose against their oppressors, the Spaniards. The rebel army besieged Lima, the capital of Peru.

Fearful for their wealth, their vast accumulation of gold and silver, and their Churches' rich ornaments, the Spaniards sought to send them to Spain for safety. They asked a man named Boag to find a ship, and he went to the port of Callao on the coast. In the harbour lay the *Mary Dear*, whose English Captain, Thompson, was known and trusted by the Spaniards. That they put their treasures on the English ship is a historical fact, vouched for by the British Admiral, Cochrane, who then commanded the Spanish South American fleet.

The *Mary Dear* sailed from Callao carrying the treasures of Lima, with an escort of six soldiers, two priests and Boag. Within a few days the gold-crazy crew murdered the guards, seized the ship, and sailed her to Cocos Island, where they concealed the treasure. Its bulk was hidden in a cave.

There is great mystery about this cave. The crew of the *Mary Dear* seem to have found a ready-made hiding place. This cave, in a cliff face, was barred by a secret door, fitting so close into the rock that it could not be seen. It could be opened by putting an iron bar into a tiny crevice and levering it outwards. The cave, it is thought, had been made by the ancient Peruvians, skilled workers in stone and able to voyage hundreds of miles on their balsa rafts.

The mutineers, having hidden their loot, sailed the *Mary Dear* to Panama. The hue and cry for the treasure thieves had already reached that Spanish city, and they were arrested and thrown into prison. Only Captain Thompson, the Mate, James Forbes, and Boag escaped execution. On their promise to lead the Spaniards to the treasure, Thompson and Forbes were taken to Cocos. They escaped from their guards and hid in the thick jungle. The Spaniards gave up the search for them after a few weeks, believing that no one could escape from that remote island. Thompson and Forbes lived on the island for a year before they were rescued by a passing ship and taken to the mainland.

27

Overleaf: Uneasy scene aboard the *Mary Dear* just before the crew murdered the guards and seized the ship carrying the treasure of Lima.

Forbes then went to live in California, while Thompson returned to the sea. Some years later Thompson became friendly with another seaman named John Keating, to whom he disclosed the secret hiding-place of the treasure. He gave Keating a map and instructions how to find the cave. Of Keating we know only that he came from Newfoundland.

Thompson then disappears from the story, but the mysterious Boag reappears. He and Keating met and sailed together to Cocos in a ship named the *Edgecombe*. They went ashore alone, but they had aroused the suspicions and greed of the crew by their unguarded talk of treasure. When they returned to the ship with their pockets full of gold, they were forced to promise that they would share their treasure. That night Keating and Boag slipped ashore. Like their predecessors, Thompson and Forbes, they hid in the jungle, and the *Edgecombe* sailed without them; she was lost with all hands rounding stormy Cape Horn.

Some time later Keating was picked up by a passing ship. He told a sad story: poor Boag had been drowned. But on his return to Newfoundland, Keating told a different story: he and Boag had found the treasure cave; he had knocked Boag on the head and left him within. He had taken some gold ($110,000, he said), but had been forced to leave the bulk of it in the cave, with Boag's body. Keatings's wife watched him in his room, through a chink in the curtains, counting piles of gold.

Before he died, in 1882, Keating gave his secret to three people:

Chatham Bay, Cocos Islands.

his wife, a man named Fred Hackett, and his servant, Nicholas Fitzgerald. He told each beneficiary that he or she alone possessed the true secret of the hiding-place of the treasure, and that he had given the others false information.

Which of these three people inherited the true map of Cocos? Fitzgerald claimed that it was he, as Keating would not have given it to his wife, whom he hated.

Mrs Keating then teamed up with Fred Hackett. They sailed to Cocos, searched the island, but found no treasure. Hackett returned alone several years later with equal lack of success. He then gave his map to other people.

The mainstream of the Keating legend descends from Fitzgerald. He did not visit Cocos, but gave his map in turn to two Englishmen.

The first man, the British Admiral Henry Palliser, stopped his ship at Cocos and landed 300 sailors whom he set to work, blasting, digging and tunnelling. His secret visit to another nation's territory led to a reprimand from the Admiralty. Palliser then returned privately with an army officer named Hervey de Montmorency. They quarrelled, and their row ended in a scuffle in which shots were fired and a man was killed. The story was enlarged into a 'battle' by the world's newspapers. As a result, since then, the Costa Rican government, which owns the island, has insisted that all treasure hunters must be accompanied by a platoon of soldiers.

Pallisser tried to follow Fitzgerald's instructions. He landed in the bay on the north-east of the island (Chatham Bay), followed the creek inland to where he saw a gap in the hills ahead, turned north and crossed a stream. According to the map, he would then find himself facing a steep cliff. In its face, at shoulder height, he would find a tiny crevice, in which to place an iron bar. When levered outwards, the door would turn, disclosing the cave. Within he would find coins, gold bars, jewels, a life-size golden statue of the Virgin Mary – and, of course, Boag's skeleton.

But there was no cliff, only a huge pile of rock and earth. Palliser and de Montmorency gave up in despair.

Fitzgerald's copy of Keating's map cropped up again in 1926. It came into the possession of Sir Malcolm Campbell, the land- and water-speed record holder. He visited Cocos on a friend's yacht. His companions became impatient, expecting him to find the treasure in a couple of days, but Campbell failed to interpret Fitzgerald's clues and sailed away.

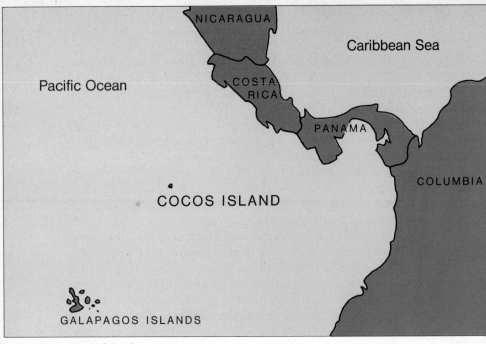

Cocos Island.

Dozens, possibly hundreds, of other treasure hunters have sought the Cocos treasures. August Gissler, a German seaman, told a strange tale. During his seafaring career he met a man who had sailed on the *Mary Dear*. He told Gissler where the treasure had been hidden – buried in the ground but not in a cave. Gissler lived on Cocos for twenty years. He traced many clues but found no treasures.

Keating found treasure in a cave. That is the only certain fact. No one has found that cave again, as far as is known. Successful treasure hunters keep quiet about their finds.

Two friends of mine have visited Cocos. They believe that the famous cave, and its rich contents, and perhaps deposits elsewhere, can only be located by the use of powerful metal detectors. Even so, to mount a full-scale search would cost huge sums of money. Heavy earth-moving machinery would need to be landed, and the island has no piers or wharfs. Still, it would seem worth the risk.

In the cathedral at Lima stands an empty niche. It once housed the golden statue of the Virgin Mary – the same golden statue which Keating saw in the Cocos cave.

The Oak Island Mystery

Had I not seen it for myself, I doubt if I would have believed it. It is a maddening yet fascinating mystery. I have visited the island twice and have written a book about the 177-year search for treasure on Oak Island, Nova Scotia, Canada's Atlantic Province.

The treasure hunt began by chance in 1795 when three local boys landed on the tiny, uninhabited island in Mahonne Bay. Walking over it they found a wide clearing in the oak trees, at its centre one gnarled and ancient oak. A branch 16 feet (4·8 metres) above ground, had been lopped short. Below it the ground had sunk into a saucer-like depression. Someone had once dug there; and why would anyone dig there but to bury treasure?

Fetching tools from their homes across the bay, the boys started to dig beneath the oak tree. They did not get far, before they called in helpers who continued the excavation. This is what they and their successors discovered:

The shaft is 13 feet (3·9 m) wide and 175 feet (34·1 m) deep. At each 10 feet (3 m) level to 90 feet (27·4 m) the excavators found and lifted out oaken platforms stretching across the width of the shaft. Several of these platforms were sealed with layers of ship's putty.

At 90 feet (27·4 m) the treasure hunters unearthed a flat stone, inscribed with strange letters. They have been deciphered to read ' Forty feet below two million '. Eight feet (2·4 m) further down their picks struck an obstruction in the soil which was becoming noticeably wet. They went home that night rejoicing, believing that only a few hours' digging lay between them and the treasure. Coming back next morning, they found the shaft filled with water to within 33 feet (10 m) of the top. No amount of bailing or pumping could lower it.

They then put down drills. These *appeared* to disclose the presence at 98 feet (30·1 m) of two oak chests. The drill wobbled as it went through them. Its strange behaviour suggested that the bits were pushing aside coins.

They dug another shaft alongside the first, which they named the 'Money Pit'. Reaching 98 feet (30·1 m) they tunnelled sideways. Then the old shaft collapsed, carrying the 'chests' into the watery depths below.

But where did the water that flooded the Money Pit come from? The source was discovered by chance – a treasure hunter fell in. The water tasted salty, and so it could be carried to the Money Pit only by a subterranean tunnel.

Searching the beach at the little landing cove provided the amazing answer. 'They' – the men who had dug the Money Pit – had harnessed the tides of the Atlantic Ocean to guard it. They had built a giant sponge, a water catchment, on the beach, 145 feet (44 m) long and 5 feet (1·5 m) deep. It entrapped and held each high tide. Then five drains carried the water to a sump-hole above the tunnel.

By digging downwards and taking out the oaken platforms in the Money Pit, the treasure hunters had turned on the tap and released the water stored in the 500-feet (152·4 m) long tunnel.

From its discovery in 1850 until now, this ingenious flooding

Sketch map of Oak Island showing the position of the money pit.

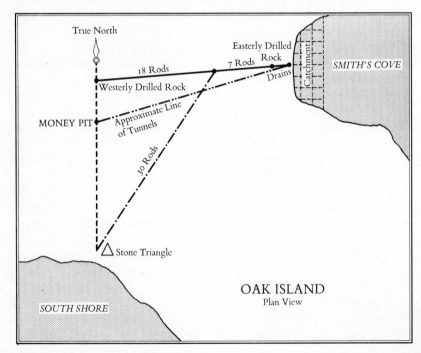

system has defeated hosts of treasure hunters. Its existence has excited rather than depressed them. The buried treasure must be vast to have required such amazing safeguards.

The treasure hunters rose to the new challenge. They built a huge coffer dam on the beach to hold back the sea, but it was washed away by an unusually high tide. They found and dynamited one flood tunnel, but the water in the Money Pit remained at tide level, 33 feet (10 m) from the top. This proved the existence of a second, lower tunnel. The high tunnel enters the Money Pit at 110 feet (33·5 m), the lower one at 150 feet (45·7 m).

The treasure hunters spent fifty years digging and tunnelling around the Money Pit and by the landing cove, trying to find and block these flood tunnels. In all, twenty shafts were dug, and hundreds of feet of tunnels were run; but the water in the Money Pit remained at tide level.

The treasure hunters as they came and went appear to have thought of everything. Several engineers planned to freeze the mud and slush which filled the Money Pit. One hoped to lower an iron caisson – a metal tube which would enclose the shaky sides of the shaft and prevent its collapse. Another tried to descend, wearing a diver's suit. Still others searched on the island for the 'water-gate' which they believed could be used to stop the flooding. Most treasure hunters tried drilling into the watery depths of the Money Pit.

This drilling disclosed what some people believe to be an iron-and-cement, water-tight treasure vault lying between 150 feet (45·7 m) and 175 feet (53·3 m). The wish may have been father to the thought. Others think that the obstruction they struck at these depths is the 'chests' which had dropped when the Money Pit collapsed.

Except for one tiny piece of parchment and the cipher stone nothing has been brought up from the depths of the Money Pit. But why else was it dug? Why did it require such extraordinary safeguards?

Some time before 1795 a gang of men spent months on the island, digging and tunnelling, for some purpose. What else than to conceal treasure?

Was the Money Pit dug as a blind to distract attention from other places on the island? 'They' left their shaft obvious to see, its site marked by an ancient oak tree, its branch lopped short, clear

Aerial view of Oak Island, showing (centre) the Money Pit area.

indication that it had been used as a hoist. They could have up-rooted the tree and let it fall across their shaft. Chance visitors would have concluded it had been blown down in a storm, and the Money Pit might never have been found.

I think that someone buried treasure on Oak Island, but not in the inaccessible depths of the Money Pit. Other discoveries made on the island suggest that several caches of treasure may lie buried.

A treasure seeker in 1937 made an exciting discovery – or rather several discoveries. In an old book he found a code – a 'stepping-out' course which ran thus:

18 W and 7 E on Rock
30 S W
14 N Tree
7 by 8 by 4.

His partner had noticed two rocks, each with a drilled hole. They were set 25 rods apart, the sum of 18 plus 7. Stepping out the course, they went '30' rods 'S.W.'. In a clump of bushes they found a stone triangle. Through it ran an arrow of stones. It pointed due north directly at the Money Pit.

The next stage of the directions, '14 N Tree', fell far short of the site of the Money Pit, a confusion which no one has been able to explain satisfactorily. What the figures '7 by 8 by 4' mean is anyone's guess. They may mean a triangle formed of those dimensions. This is the important fact. Someone laid out a marker system and devised a code to fit it. They did that in order to provide themselves with a way back to their treasure cache or caches. Did they return to dig up their treasure?

One spot on the island shows signs of digging. I believe that 'they' did return, but only to recover one of several separate treasure caches. One or more may remain, awaiting discovery by the man who can interpret the code and fit it to the markers, the two drilled rocks and the stone triangle.

Who were 'they'? Pirates are the popular choice. But it seems unlikely that pirates would have spent months digging and tunnelling on the island. They were notorious spendthrifts, and they would not have had the skill to construct such amazing engineering works. The theory of pirate origin is, however, supported by the name of the bay in which Oak Island lies. The French word *mahonne* described a low-lying, fast type of sailing ship, much used by pirates in the Mediterranean Sea.

Many other guesses have been made. One investigator believes that a disabled Spanish galleon put into, or was wrecked in, Mahonne Bay. Rather than risk the Atlantic voyage to Spain, her captain hid the gold and silver ingots on Oak Island. Another investigator believes that the Money Pit contains the lost manuscripts of Shakespeare's plays. This, he thinks, is proved by a piece of parchment brought up from its depths.

It is even harder to find an answer to the question 'Why?' The coast of Mahonne Bay did not become inhabited until 1759. Thereby hangs a strange story. One of the settlers told the boys who found the Money Pit in 1795 that the people of Chester, the little town four miles across the bay, had seen lights and fires at night on the island. A boat-load of men had rowed over to investigate and had never returned.

Another strange discovery has been made on the island. In 1971 the searchers decided to probe the ground to learn what lay beneath. They sank a shaft 26 inches (600 mm) wide. Five divers descended to 235 feet (71·6 m). They found themselves in a huge cavern which extends beneath the Money Pit. This is probably a 'solution cavern', as it is called, a huge underground cavity formed by the action of water often found in limestone formations. It, too,

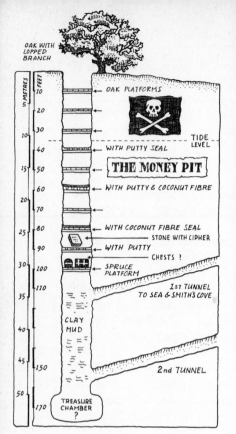

OAK WITH
LOPPED
BRANCH

← OAK PLATFORMS

TIDE LEVEL

WITH PUTTY SEAL

THE MONEY PIT

← WITH PUTTY & COCONUT FIBRE

← WITH COCONUT FIBRE SEAL
——— STONE WITH CIPHER
← WITH PUTTY
——— CHESTS ?

SPRUCE PLATFORM

1st TUNNEL
TO SEA & SMITH'S COVE

CLAY MUD

2nd TUNNEL

TREASURE CHAMBER ?

Left: Diagram of the Money Pit.
Above: The south shore excavations of the Money Pit, 1965.

is flooded by a man-made tunnel which brings water from the beach.

When I visited the island for the second time in 1967 the ground around the Money Pit had been devastated. The recent searchers had excavated huge craters in their attempts to block the flood tunnels. Four men died there in 1965 in the shaft they were digging near the landing cove. The fumes from their water-pump suffocated them. In all, I reckon, something like $1,500,000 have been spent on the island in a vain attempt to find a treasure which may not exist. The island will give up its secret, the local people say, when its last oak tree has gone. Only two remain. They lie toppled amongst the spruce trees which have replaced the once luxuriant growth of oaks.

For further reading:
Rupert Furneaux, *The Money Pit Mystery*, Tom Stacey, 1972.

Inca Gold

When the Spaniards conquered Peru in the early fifteen hundreds, they stole and shipped to Spain vast treasures, the huge store of gold collected by the Inca kings, but modern treasure hunters believe that the Incas, the rulers of Peru, hid far more gold than was taken from them. The last Inca king, Atahualpa, to secure his freedom, offered to fill the room in which he stood with gold to shoulder height, and at his order gold trains set out to bring the ransom to his capital. But the greedy Spaniards became impatient and murdered him before the room had been half filled. Hearing of their king's death, the Indians took the rest of the ransom and hid it in the mountains. 'There are countless treasures in this country, but only a miracle can bring them to light', remarked the conqueror's brother, Pedro Pizarro.

Modern treasure hunters await the miracle. According to the legend the bulk of the treasure, worth perhaps £50,000,000, was hidden in mountain caves and lakes. Several caches were made in and around Cuzco, the Inca capital. The legends follow the same pattern. Knowledge of these hiding places has descended in Indian families, but their modern descendants still will not tell where they lie. Perhaps in the past some Indians may have talked.

The Indian wife of a Spanish soldier said in 1557 that part of the treasure had been thrown into Lake Urcos, near Cuzco. The Spaniards drained the lake, and the soldier suddenly became rich.

Several European 'botanists' in the nineteenth century made their hobby an excuse for treasure hunting. They picked up stories from the natives and spent months searching for long-forgotten lakes in the Andes mountains. Others spent their life-times searching for caves.

Another famous legend concerns 'Eldorado' – the Gilded Man. For once legend spoke the truth. Before the Spanish Conquest the tribe who lived on the lofty tableland of Bogota, in the modern republic of Columbia, followed an ancient custom. Once each year the Chief covered his body with sticky gum and gold dust. The tribesmen took him to the centre of the lake into which he plunged,

and the water washed the gold from his body. His subjects cast their offerings, gold and emeralds, into the lake.

The story of the gold-encrusted king excited the Spaniards, and two expeditions travelled to Lake Quatavila in 1538. They cut a channel to drain it, reducing the water level by seventy-five feet, and they recovered golden objects valued at $850,000.

After the Spaniards left the Indians revived the ancient ceremony in the belief that the Spaniards would think that they had found all the treasure and would not return. They never did. The Indians were left in peace for 250 years; then the English naval chaplain, Charles Stuart Cochrane, heard that the Indians 'had cast as much gold as 50 men could carry' into the lake. His words were read by a British group of treasure hunters, and in 1903 they again drained the lake by piercing the hill with a tunnel 1,100 feet (335·2 m) long. Before they could dig its depths, the thick deposit of silt hardened to rock-like concrete under the sun's rays, and, unable to dig through it, they gave up and went away. Within a few years the lake refilled.

Another Peruvian treasure hunt concerns the Jesuit missionaries who built a monastery at Plazuela, in the valley of Sacambaya. Having established their mission in 1635, 'the Holy Fathers grew tired of converting the heathen', and before long the valley became the scene of their rapidly expanding mining activities. For over a hundred years the priests hoarded their riches. When they were faced with expulsion in 1778 they concealed their gold in a cave hollowed out of the Caballo Cunco hill.

One priest noted directions. His paper was passed down in a Peruvian family, the last of whom gave it to the English explorer, Cecil Prodgers. The directions instructed him to climb to the top of the hill, where he would find a big stone shaped like an egg. If he dug beneath it he would come to the roof of the cave, so large that it had taken 500 Indians two-and-a-half years to hollow it out. Amongst other treasures, he would find an image of the Madonna, made of pure gold, three feet high, the eyes of which were two large diamonds. Great care, the paper warned, needed to be taken in the cave as enough poison had been left there to kill a regiment.

Prodgers did not go on a search himself, but gave the paper to another explorer, Edgar Sanders. In 1926 Sanders discovered the mouth of a tunnel at the foot of the hill. Within this tunnel he found ancient writing – carved or painted on the rock – warning

41

Opposite: 'Eldorado', the gilded man.

anyone who entered of their possible fate. His native workers refused to go farther. Sanders returned with several other Englishmen in 1928, and they set to work to remove the 'egg-shaped' boulder on the top of the hill. Beneath it they found and followed a maze of tunnels which led into the heart of the hill. One hundred feet from the top they reached a domed chamber from which radiated more tunnels, but they failed to find the fabled cavern in which 'lay buried twelve million pounds' worth of gold'. Another treasure hunt in the Sacambaya valley led by two Englishmen in 1967 was equally unsuccessful.

Thus, like the Inca gold, the Jesuit treasure awaits discovery.

For further reading:
A. F. Bandelier, *The Gilded Man*, 1901.
C. M. Dyott, *Man Hunting in the Jungle*, Edward Arnold, 1930.
James Stead, *Treasure Trek*, Routledge, 1936.
M. Howell and T. Morrison, *Steps to a Fortune*, 1967.

The Seychelles Treasure

We know little about Olivier de Vasseur other than that he was a French pirate who preyed upon ships in the Indian Ocean. He made two rich captures, the Portuguese vessel, *Vierge du Cap,* carrying the Viceroy and the Archbishop of Goa, the Portuguese colony on the Indian coast, and an Arab ship. She carried a princess on her way to marry in Zanzibar, on the coast of Africa. Both vessels were transporting rich cargoes of gold, silver and jewels.

De Vasseur's own ship, *Le Victorieux,* was captured by the French frigate *Mèduse.* He was taken to the island of Réunion, where he was hanged on 17 July, 1730. From the scaffold de Vasseur tossed a paper to the spectators, crying 'Find my treasure who can!' The paper proved to be a chart, with directions how to find the treasure he had hidden in a cave in the Seychelles Islands.

This chart came into the possession of a family named Savy who lived on the island of Mahé, one of the Seychelles group. These islands became a British colony in 1814.

The chart led the Savy family to the beach at Bel Ombre. They found other papers in the Archives at Mauritius. Few people have seen these papers, and we are told only that they contain a cryptogram.

The Savy family dug the beach at Bel Ombre between 1913 and 1923. An old man, it is reported, adept at cryptograms, spent twenty years studying these signs and symbols without arriving at any solution. A cryptogram is another way of describing a cipher, but with one difference: a cryptogram uses signs and symbols rather than letters and words. To interpret a cryptogram it is necessary to 'see into the mind' of the person who drew it. That is why our ignorance of de Vasseur is so galling.

The search for de Vasseur's treasure might have ended had not an Englishman arrived in the Seychelles in 1948. This man, Reginald Herbert Cruise-Wilkins, had been an officer in the Guards and had been living in Kenya, in East Africa, for some years. He visited the Seychelles on holiday without realizing that he would have to wait three months for a boat to take him back to East Africa. He went to stay at Bel Ombre, where he met Mrs Charles Savy and the man who had been working on the cryptogram. They showed him the chart and pointed out on the beach rocks and cliffs on which had been drawn pictures of dogs, serpents, tortoises, horses, and human beings. Cruise-Wilkins was hooked. The more he studied the cryptogram and these rock markings, the more convinced he became that they formed a crude code invented to show the place de Vasseur had hidden his treasure. 'My first study of the documents convinced me,' he told a visitor in 1967, 'that the plan for burying the treasure had been based on stories from Greek mythology, and on the position of the stars'. De Vasseur, he thought, had devised a game to 'befuddle' those who might seek to find his treasure.

If Cruise-Wilkins is right, de Vasseur must have been a very well-read pirate. He had based his cryptogram on the Seven Labours of Hercules. For example, Hercules had been given the task of killing the water-snake, Hydra. De Vasseur, Cruise-Wilkins, believed, had used this classical parallel to explain that he had had to divert an underground stream to protect his treasure cavern. Another rock carving depicted the goddess Andromeda, chained to a rock, waiting to be devoured by a monster.

Early in his search, Cruise-Wilkins realized that much money

would be required to pay the cost of excavating the beach at Bel Ombre, so he returned to Kenya where he raised £24,000.

Back at Bel Ombre again, he learned that Mrs Savy had found that six compass bearings given on the chart intersected on the beach at a certain point. She and her helpers had unearthed two coffins containing skeletons and another body, possibly the remains of the pirates de Vasseur had killed to prevent their disclosing the secret of the treasure's hiding place.

Cruise-Wilkins has been digging and tunnelling on the beach at Bel Ombre since 1950. Two visitors found him at work in 1952 and 1967. The first watched a professional mineral diviner scanning the sand with rods and 'something that looked like a ping-pong ball on the end of a string'. The surrounding hills echoed to the sounds of blasting and a small gang of Negroes were busy digging holes. They were searching, he was told, for the supposed cave which was believed to lie beneath a great area of granite rock.

The second visitor, fifteen years later, found the beach honeycombed with man-made tunnels which ran below sea level. A high stone wall had been built to hold back the sea. Cruise-Wilkins told him that getting at the cavern, in which the treasure was supposed to lie, was a massive and dangerous engineering job. The cavern is protected by a huge slab of rock and is guarded by the sea. It can be approached only from one direction, which is indicated by three stones depicting the Golden Apples of the Hesperides, another ancient Greek myth.

Opposite page: De Vasseur tossed his chart from the scaffold crying 'Find my treasure who can'.

Right: An aerial view of Port Launay, Mahé, in the Seychelles Islands.

Left: Morning, Anse aux Pins, Mahé.

The entrance to the treasure cave is many feet underground, possibly beneath an overhanging rock, and is protected by man-made tunnels which carry the sea to flood it, should the searcher attempt to enter it from the wrong and the dangerous direction.

'De Vasseur has led me almost in a complete circle', Cruise-Wilkins told his visitor. 'But I believe that at last I have him.' Wisely, Cruise-Wilkins is disinclined to describe his progress, as I found in 1972 when I corresponded with him.

Cruise-Wilkins believes that the treasure is contained in three chests, each about seven feet long and three feet wide. Almost more interesting is his description of how he thinks de Vasseur looked. He pictures him as a small man with a limp. He was nick-named La Buse, the Buzzard.

Cruise-Wilkins is still digging and tunnelling. Whether or not he finds treasure, he will have spent twenty or more exciting years, occupied by a hobby which has become an obsession. That is the way of treasure hunting.

For further reading:
F. D. Ommaney, *The Shoals of Capricorn*, Longmans, 1952.
Athol Thomas, *Forgotten Eden*, 1968.

Other Famous Treasures Lost and Found

The Tower of London

About £7,000 supposed to have been hidden in the basement of the White Tower by Colonel John Barkstead during the time of Oliver Cromwell. Searched for by the diarist, Samuel Pepys, and again in 1957.

King John's Regalia

That King John lost his Crown and Sceptre 'in the Wash', the East Coast estuary, is one of the myths of history, but the Royal

Regalia was used at the coronation of his successor, Henry III. John's army was cut off by the incoming tide, and he may have lost some of his baggage.

The Vigo Galleons

The British Admiral Sir George Rooke pursued the Spanish plate fleet into Vigo Bay (on the western coast of Spain) on 23 October 1702. The sunken galleons are supposed to have carried treasure valued at £24,651,323. Tremendous efforts have been made to locate and raise them. Even Jules Verne (*Twenty Thousand Leagues Under the Sea*) brought Captain Nemo in the *Nautilus* into the bay, where the crew picked up 'ingots of gold and silver, cascades of piastres and jewels'. Alas, Jules Verne was romancing. The long succession of treasure hunters have found nothing, probably because the Spaniards had time to unload the galleons before the British fleet swept into the bay.

Le Chameau

This French pay ship sank off the coast of Cape Breton Island (part of Canada's Atlantic Province), on 26 August 1725. She carried 300,000 gold and silver coins. In 1966 three young Canadians found the wreck and recovered coins which were valued at £90,000.

The Association

Admiral Sir Cloudsley Shovell's flagship, the *Association*, was wrecked on the Scilly Islands on 22 October 1702. Three other battleships of his squadron also struck the Gilstone Reef. Since 1967 two teams of skin-divers have been working on these wrecks. Roland Morris from Penzance has recovered 1,500 gold and silver coins. Another million pounds' worth, he believes, lies scattered on the seabed.

Old Basing House, Hampshire

The fifth Marquis of Winchester, it is believed, concealed plate and money during the three-year siege of the house by the

Roundheads in the Civil War. The house is now scheduled as an ancient monument and digging is not allowed.

Lost Galleons

Teddy Tucker of Bermuda is said to have recovered treasure worth $150,000 from two galleons lost on the reefs, the *San Pedro* in 1595, and the *San Antonio* in 1621. Jack Slack of the Bahamas is said to have found an un-named galleon there. Harry E. Rieseberg (*I Dive For Treasure*, 1942) claims to have found $135,000 in Caribbean wrecks.

The Tobermory Galleon

When the Spanish Armada was dispersed in 1588, the surviving ships attempted to sail around Scotland. One galleon entered and sank in Tobermory Bay. She is said to have been the *Florencia*, the Armada's pay ship. Despite extensive diving by individuals and teams she has not been located, due (as one of the divers told me) to the hundreds of tons of sand under which her wreck may lie.

Jean Lafitte

The long search for the treasure believed to have been hidden on Galveston island, Texas, by the nineteenth-century hero-pirate, Jean Lafitte, has not yet achieved success.

The Nazi Loot

Long search in the depths of Lake Toplitz in Austria and off the coast of Corsica, the Mediterranean island, for the treasures supposedly hidden by the Nazis in 1945, has not, as far as is known, produced results. But the Nazi treasure is a 'forbidden' subject: those who know about it keep silent.